W9-AVK-106

ADVENTURES OF THE
WEB-SLINGER

Written by Simon Hugo

Editorial Assistant Beth Davies
Designer Sam Bartlett
Senior Editor Hannah Dolan
Pre-Production Producer Marc Staples
Producer Isabell Schart
Managing Editor Paula Regan
Managing Art Editor Guy Harvey
Art Director Lisa Lanzarini
Publisher Julie Ferris
Publishing Director Simon Beecroft

Reading Consultant Linda Gambrell, PhD.

The author would like to thank Ned Hartley and Mark McKenzie-Ray
for their assistance.

First American Edition, 2016
Published in the United States by DK Publishing
345 Hudson Street, New York, New York 10014
DK, a Division of Penguin Random House LLC

16 17 18 19 20 10 9 8 7 6 5 4 3 2 1

001–291444–Apr/2016

marvelkids.com

©2016 MARVEL

All rights reserved.
Without limiting the rights under the copyright reserved above,
no part of this publication may be reproduced, stored in or introduced
into a retrieval system, or transmitted, in any form, or by any means
(electronic, mechanical, photocopying, recording, or otherwise),
without the prior written permission of the copyright owner.
Published in Great Britain by Dorling Kindersley Limited.

DK books are available at special discounts when purchased in bulk for sales
promotions, premiums, fund-raising, or educational use. For details, contact: DK
Publishing Special Markets, 345 Hudson Street, New York, New York 10014
SpecialSales@dk.com

A catalog record for this book is available
from the Library of Congress.

ISBN: 978-1-4654-5161-3 (Hardback)
ISBN: 978-1-4654-5160-6 (Paperback)

Printed and bound in China.

www.dk.com

A WORLD OF IDEAS
SEE ALL THERE IS TO KNOW

Contents

4   Introduction
6   **Peter Parker**
8   School Report
20 Bugle Buzz
22 **With Great Power...**
24 Suiting Up
30 *Daily Bugle*
34 Suit Scrapbook
36 **Terrible Foes**
38 Harry and Norman
44 Sinister Six

56 **Amazing Allies**
60 *Daily Bugle* Online
66 Avengers Briefing
70 **Great Responsibilities**
74 The Divide
80 **World of Spiders**
86 Spider-verse Heroes
90 Quiz
92 Glossary
94 Index and Quiz Answers

Introduction

Spider-Man is the friendly neighborhood hero with the powers of a super spider. He can climb up walls, spin sticky webs, and swing between buildings without even breaking a sweat. He uses his powers to fight crime and to save people who are in danger.

Spider-Man wears a mask to stop his enemies from finding out who he really is. Only a handful of his closest friends and fellow Super Heroes know that his real name is Peter Parker—and that underneath the mask there is a young man trying to live an ordinary life.

There is nothing ordinary about Peter's life, however. Ever since he was bitten by a radioactive spider, he has been the hero at the heart of one amazing adventure after another. He has super strength and speed, but he also has a brilliant brain, and likes to use his scientific skills whenever he can.

If he sets out to stop a Super Villain's plot, the bad guys should fear Peter's mind as much as Spidey's muscles.

Spider-Man has many friends and many enemies. He has battled monsters and saved the world from Super Villains. He has made tough choices and lost loved ones. His story is far from over, but these are some of the best parts so far...

Peter Parker

Life at Midtown High School was tough for young Peter Parker. Although Peter loved to study, especially science, he was shy and found it difficult to make friends. He was not strong or good at sports, and some of his classmates called him "Puny Parker." No one wished they had super-powers more than Peter!

Peter lived with his Aunt May and Uncle Ben. His mother and father had died a long time ago, and he was too young to remember much about them.

Peter loved his aunt and uncle very much, and they cared for him more than anyone else in the world. They encouraged Peter in his studies, and were always there to comfort him after a rough day at school. Peter hoped that his life would be different one day—but that Aunt May and Uncle Ben would never change!

SCHOOL REPORT

Peter is a highly intelligent individual. However, his school report card shows he has his strengths and weaknesses—just like everyone else.

M H S **Midtown High School**

· REPORT CARD ·

NAME: Peter Parker

GRADE: 9th

TEACHER: Raymond Warren

CLASS: A-15

TEACHER'S NOTES:

Peter is a bright boy, who excels in Math and Science. He also has a strong creative flair—photography is clearly a passion for him. Peter is a quiet member of the class, who sometimes struggles with confidence. If Peter can improve his self-confidence, he will go far.

Raymond Warren

CLASS	GRADE	NOTES
MATH	A+	With his grasp of complex systems, Peter could become a web designer.
ENGLISH	A	Peter loves to read— especially comics. It's a shame his handwriting is so spidery.
SCIENCE	A+	Peter's best subject! If he keeps this up, he's sure to get into a good school.
ART	B	Peter's flair for photography is matched by his talent for costume design.
GYM	F	Mr. Parker will never be an athlete. He has all the strength of a little bug!

No matter what else was happening (or not happening) in Peter's life, he still loved his studies. Finding out about the wonders of science was his way of escaping from the everyday world. So when he heard about an event called "Experiments in Radioactivity", he had to see what it was all about.

The event was held in a real laboratory, where scientists were showing off the power of radioactive rays. No one saw when a tiny spider got in the way of one of the rays. The unlucky spider was now radioactive, and it reacted to the shock in the only way it knew how: by biting the nearest living thing!

Peter Parker was the nearest living thing, and he began to feel very strange straight away. On his way home, he was nearly hit by a passing car. When he jumped to avoid it, he went further than he had ever jumped before. In fact, he had landed halfway up the side of a tall building!

Peter felt confused by the strange things that were happening to him. His whole body was bursting with energy, and he could climb up walls just as easily as he could walk down a street. When he crushed a metal pipe in his hand without even trying, he realized that the spider's bite had changed him. He had been given amazing powers!

Peter soon started to think about what he could use his awesome new abilities for. He realized that his days of being "Puny Parker" were at an end and that no one  would be able to laugh at him anymore. The unbelievable powers that had alarmed him at first could be his ticket to fame and fortune. He would make himself a spider suit and invent a way to spin his own webs. He would become a Spider-Man!

Peter wanted a real test of his strength and speed, so he put on a mask and entered a contest to fight with a powerful wrestler. A big crowd watched as Peter won the fight easily, and it wasn't long before he was given the chance to show off his skills on TV.

For his first television appearance, Peter dressed in his full spider suit and gave the audience a glimpse of just what he could do with his homemade web shooters. He didn't want to use his powers for a good reason. He just wanted to be famous.

Spider-Man's TV show was an instant hit and everyone wanted to see more. As Peter left the TV studio, he had to deal with talent scouts and

newspaper reporters who all wanted to talk to the man inside the spider suit.

But they were not the only people that Peter saw backstage. He also came face-to-face with a crook who was running away from a security guard. Peter had the chance to stop him, but he let him get away. He was sick of having problems to deal with. From now on, he just wanted an easy life.

Spider-Man became a celebrity after his first TV appearance, and Peter was kept busy putting on shows for adoring fans. Though his success had gone to his head, he still thought of his Aunt May and Uncle Ben. He promised himself that he would do all he could to make them both happy and support them as they had supported him.

One day, after a successful Spidey show, Peter came home to terrible news. Uncle Ben was dead. A burglar had broken into their home and Ben had surprised him. A police officer told Peter where the burglar was hiding out and Peter didn't even wait to see Aunt May. He threw on his Spider-Man suit and went to find the guilty man.

Peter tracked down the burglar and beat him easily in a fight. He was shocked to see that it was the same man who had run past him at the TV studio. If Peter had stopped the crook when he first had the chance, his Uncle Ben would still be alive.

After the death of his uncle, Peter had to face up to what being a hero really meant. If he wanted to use the great powers he had been given, he had no choice but to accept great responsibility as well. His first duty was to care for his Aunt May, who needed him now more than ever. He also had to think about all the good things that he could do as a Super Hero.

Peter turned his back on TV fame and started to use his powers to fight crime. He snared small-time crooks in his web before they could cause more trouble. He even began to battle Super Villains such as the Vulture, Sandman, and Doctor Octopus. Being a hero wasn't the easy life that Peter had imagined when he first put on his Spidey suit, but he knew that it was the right thing to do with his new gifts.

It was a new start for Spider-Man—but it wasn't the end for Peter Parker. In fact, his story was just beginning...

Spider-Man has swapped showbiz to take on villains like Electro.

WHO IS SPIDER-MAN?

Everyone has seen him on TV, and now he's started fighting crime. Some of us have even seen him swinging over our heads. Who is the man beneath the spider mask? We went to the streets to see what YOU think!

A Bugle Buzz magazine
SPECIAL
investigation!

"He's so cool! I bet he's someone famous like... the President!"
Beth, clerk.

"He must be a crook, or why would he hide his face?"
John, publisher.

"You want to know who Spidey is? I'm Spidey!"
Flash, student.

"Whoever he is, I hope he's careful not to hurt anybody."
May, retired.

"I think he sounds like a pretty cool guy!"
Peter, student.

With Great Power...

It only took a moment for that spider to bite Peter Parker, but it took a long time for the troubled teen to fully understand the amazing powers he had been given. In fact, he's still finding out new things about himself.

Spider-Man's ability to crawl up the side of buildings takes concentration. He had to teach himself to use this power carefully, otherwise he would stick to everything! He also had to learn to master the spider-sense that alerts him to nearby danger.

At first, this spider-sense was just an odd feeling in the back of his mind, but now it is a vital part of his daily battle against crime.

One power that the spider's bite did not give Peter was the ability to spin webs. That was something he had to invent for himself, using his scientific skills to create web shooters that he can wear on his wrists.

With these skills and powers under his control, and with a cool costume to wear, Peter can be confident that when his spider-sense tingles, he will be ready for whatever adventures the day has in store for him!

SUITING UP

Peter made his Spidey suit in his bedroom.
He has added new technology to it over time,
but its main job is always to hide his true identity.

DRAWING UP
Peter sketched how he wanted his suit to look before he started to make it.

STITCHING UP
Peter made his first suit from old clothes and then added his own web pattern.

MASKING UP
A mask completed the costume, hiding Peter's face from the world.

GOING UP
Peter tested his suit by heading out for some well-dressed wall-crawling!

WEBBING UP
Web shooters small enough to fit under the suit were Peter's own invention.

STOCKING UP
Peter carries backup packs of web fluid in his belt, along with other gadgets.

Spidey's webs are strong enough to support his weight.

Flexible boots for climbing up walls

Latest suit made from high-tech materials

The mask makes Spider-Man's voice sound deeper than Peter Parker's.

Spidey can see out of his mirrored mask, but no one can see in!

When Spider-Man takes on a super-powered opponent, he needs more than just the ability to climb up walls. He must use the speed and strength of a spider. That might not sound very powerful, but it is extraordinary when multiplied to match the size of a man.

Spidey can break down walls with his bare hands, bend solid metal bars, and lift almost 10 tons—which is more than the weight of an elephant! He can also jump much farther than any normal human being, leaping from one side of a street to the other, or from the ground to the roof of a three-story building.

Peter can control his strength thanks to his spider-like reflexes, which work up to 40 times faster than the brain and body of an average person.

If Spidey does suffer an injury, his super-speed even extends to healing, helping him recover from serious wounds in just a few days. It all comes in handy when battling a ferocious Super Villain such as the enormous Lizard.

 Smile! Spidey might be watching. There is more to Peter Parker than just fighting crime. He also wants to live a normal life, and that means he needs a job to pay the bills. Peter is a talented photographer and takes pictures of Spider-Man that nobody else can get. Newspaper editor John Jonah Jameson hired Peter to take photographs of Spidey, not realizing that the two were one and the same!

Peter's incredible pictures soon became a regular feature of the *Daily Bugle*, showing Spider-Man and his enemies in action. Peter set up cameras to take photos as he swooped by, and went back to collect the shots after he had dealt with the villains.

The only problem was that J.J. Jameson hated Spider-Man. He used Peter's photos to sell stories telling people that Spidey was a criminal. Even when Spider-Man saved the life of Jameson's son, the newspaper boss still found a way to blame the web-slinger.

Peter needed the money, so he had no choice but to go on selling his photos to the *Bugle*. He kept on looking for another way to make a living that didn't involve Spider-Man in any way.

DAILY BUGLE

Peter sells his photographs of Spider-Man to J.J. Jameson, the editor of the *Daily Bugle* newspaper. Unfortunately for Peter, J.J. hates Spidey and reports his good deeds as crimes!

SPIDER-MAN
ENDANGERS CHILD'S LIFE

READ MORE INSIDE!

TERRIFIED BYSTANDERS shook with fear yesterday, as the masked menace known as "Spider-Man" terrorized the streets once more.

These EXCLUSIVE pictures show the horrific moments when the web-weaving pest endangered the lives of innocent civilians. With no care for those around him, Spider-Man flew through the air, just inches above the heads of law-abiding families and at least one sweet little old lady.

But that wasn't enough chaos for Spider-Man! He was later seen clutching a child near the infant's distraught mother. Word on the street was that Spider-Man was "saving the child from drowning," but this was clearly part of a sinister kidnapping plot!

The *Daily Bugle* has seen enough of these shocking scenes. We demand to know: who is the Spider-Man? And just who can stop his criminal rampage?

Peter's next jobs all made good use of his brilliant brain without relying on his powers as Spider-Man. First he became a science teacher at his old school, and then a teaching assistant at Empire State University. Peter really got a chance to shine when he went on a tour of Horizon Labs and impressed the scientists so much that they made him part of their team!

Horizon Labs is a state-of-the-art research center where genius-level inventors come up with ideas for new technology. Peter made the most of his opportunity and quickly set to work building new equipment for Spider-Man to use. Nobody at the Labs realized that Peter was Spider-Man—they all

thought he was just helping him.

Peter left Horizon Labs when his body was taken over by Doctor Octopus (see p.78). This Super Villain thought he could do a better job of being Spider-Man than Peter himself. He even set up a new business called Parker Industries while he was pretending to be Peter. When Peter was himself again, he found he had his own company to run!

As the boss of Parker Industries, Peter is able to carry on the work he started at Horizon Labs, finding new ways to stop Super Villains from causing havoc. As Spidey, he still finds time to teach as well— passing on his Super Hero knowledge to students at the Avengers Academy.

SUIT SCRAPBOOK

Peter has adapted his costume many times.
Each new suit is specially customized to help
Spider-Man succeed in his latest mission.

This book belongs to:

...... ~~Peter~~ Spider-Man ......

This is my bulletproof
suit! I made it at
Horizon Labs when
I lost my spider-
sense for a while.

I built this armored
outfit at the university.
It looked pretty cool,
but it really slowed
me down.

Stealth suit? What stealth suit? This outfit made me completely invisible. Though not in this picture, obviously!

I designed this suit to defeat the Sinister Six. It can withstand Rhino's strength and Electro's energy blasts.

This is the first disguise I ever wore. It's a bit basic, but it was good enough to beat this wrestler!

Terrible Foes

You can judge a Super Hero by the quality of his enemies—and Spider-Man has done battle with the best of the worst! From humans to aliens, it seems like there's always a new Super Villain to test Peter Parker's strength and skill.

When Peter first became Spider-Man, one criminal genius believed defeating the web-slinger would secure his place as the King of Crime. The man was Norman Osborn, a greedy businessman with a lust for power. He used a dangerous mix of chemicals to make himself stronger and smarter. Then he disguised himself as a monster he had seen in a nightmare. He called himself the Green Goblin.

As the Goblin, Norman tried to destroy Spider-Man, but he never succeeded and grew more insane with each failure. Yet as Norman Osborn, he remained a respected businessman, and used his chemically boosted brainpower to convince the world that he was the true hero.

HARRY AND NORMAN

Harry Osborn is Peter Parker's friend and Norman Osborn's son. He does not get along well with his Dad, and doesn't know that Norman is really the Super Villain known as the Green Goblin.

Inbox (1)
Contacts
Favorites
Sent Mail
Drafts
Trash

From: Harry Osborn
To: Norman Osborn
Subject: Spider-Man!

Sunday 11:37

Hi Dad,

Have you seen Peter's latest photos of Spider-Man? He really showed the Green Goblin who is best!

It's funny, I feel like you've been more distant than ever since the Green Goblin came along.

It would be really great to hear from you. The kids at college think it must be great to be the son of Norman Osborn, but I wish you had an ordinary job and weren't such a rich, important businessman.

Speak soon?

Harry

OSCORP
EMAIL

Inbox (63)
Contacts
Favorites
Sent Mail
Drafts
Trash

 From: Norman Osborn

To: Harry Osborn

Subject: Re: Spider-Man!

Friday 5:53

Harry,

You sound well. I am glad. But please remember that I don't have time to email you every week.

Do you mean the image attached below? Why are you sure that Spider-Man is the hero here? Does anyone even know who he is?

I advise you to read the *Daily Bugle* a little more often, if you wish to know the truth about Spider-Man.

As for your wish that I had an "ordinary job"... You really don't have anything to complain about! The more money I make, the better it is for you.

I have given you everything a son could want. If you are lucky, one day you will be just like me.

Regards,

N

Norman Osborn turned himself into the Green Goblin on purpose, but some Super Villains are the unlucky victims of accidents. Electro is a powerful criminal who can control electricity—draining it from cables and machines before shooting it out from his fingers and eyes. However, he was once just an ordinary man named Maxwell Dillon. Unlucky Max was struck by lightning while holding on to two power lines, leaving him buzzing with electrical energy. He realized that he could use this power as a weapon and

decided to give up his quiet life for a life of crime. Spider-Man has defeated Electro many times, but he also saved Max's life when he tried to absorb too much energy.

Just like Electro, Doctor Octopus was also created in a freak accident. But unlike Max Dillon, Otto Octavius was far from ordinary before he turned into Doc Ock.

Otto was one of the world's greatest atomic scientists. He was famous for inventing special robotic arms that let him handle dangerous materials at a safe distance. It was a chemical explosion in his laboratory that bonded him to these metal arms and gave him the power to control them with his mind.

Now that he was strong as well as smart, Doctor Octopus decided that nothing should stand in the way of his scientific research. He stole equipment and forced people to help him. He also hijacked a nuclear laboratory, and only Spider-Man was able to save the day.

When Doc Ock was sent to jail, his robot arms were taken away. Nobody knew that he could control the arms even when they weren't part of his body. He used the power of his mind to make them come and rescue him.

He grew obsessed with Spider-Man and formed a gang to work against him called the Sinister Six. He even attacked Aunt May—he kidnapped her and planned to marry her as part of his villainous plot.

THE SINISTER SIX

Doc Ock formed the Sinister Six when he realized Super Villains had to work together to bring down Spider-Man. Members have come and gone, but this latest lineup is the meanest of them all!

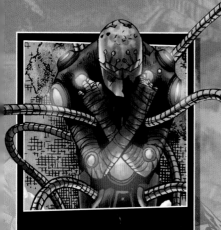

DOCTOR OCTOPUS

REAL NAME: Otto Octavius
POWERS: Controls his metal arms with his mind
ROLE: Doc Ock is a true criminal mastermind, and the driving force behind most of the Sinister Six's plans. His metal tentacles are the long arms of lawlessness!

MYSTERIO

REAL NAME: Quentin Beck
POWERS: Master of magic and illusion
ROLE: Mysterio delights in causing confusion wherever he goes. This makes it harder for Spider-Man to stop the Sinister Six—or even see them!

ELECTRO

REAL NAME: Maxwell Dillon
POWERS: Control over electrical energy and charges
ROLE: As a human battery, Electro adds a whole new level of power to the Sinister Six! This bright spark is the only member of the gang who has the ability to fly.

SANDMAN

REAL NAME: William Baker
POWERS: Can change his size, shape, and hardness
ROLE: Sandman expands the size of the Sinister Six in more ways than one! He can make himself into a giant, or spread himself out like an army.

THE CHAMELEON

REAL NAME: Dmitri Smerdyakov
POWERS: Master of disguise and mimicry
ROLE: The Chameleon helps the Sinister Six cover their tracks, pretending to be other people and making them look guilty of crimes they did not commit.

RHINO

REAL NAME: Aleksei Sytsevich
POWERS: The speed and strength of a rhinoceros
ROLE: The Rhino is not the brains of the Sinister Six, but his brute strength and inability to feel pain make him a valuable addition to any criminal gang.

Sandman is a very different kind of
villain from Doc Ock, although they both
fight in the Sinister Six. He was a cheat at
school and later became a crook. His real
name is William Baker, but he took the
nickname "Sandman" after a huge dose
of radiation blended his body with the sandy
ground beneath him, meaning that he could
change his shape as easily as if it were sand.

The first time that Spider-Man met
Sandman, he thought he was just an
ordinary criminal. However, the Super
Villain was able to make himself as hard
as rock one minute, and then literally slip
through Spider-Man's fingers the next.
The web-slinger beat him by sucking him
into a vacuum cleaner when he turned to
tiny grains of sand—but Sandman would
not fall for that trick again!

Sandman has fought Spider-Man many

times, turning
his fists into huge
hammers, or his
whole body into a
whirling sandstorm.
He has sometimes
tried to be good and
redeem himself,
but being a hero
goes against his
villainous grains.

It seems unlikely that Spider-Man and Sandman will ever be friends, but at times the terrifying monster known as the Lizard is one of Spidey's closest allies. That's because the Lizard lives inside Doctor Curt Connors—and sometimes the doctor has to live inside the Lizard.

Doctor Connors is a brilliant chemist who has helped Spider-Man find ways to stop some of the Super Villains he has faced. He also invented a way for humans to grow back lost body parts, just like some reptiles do. He tested it on himself to see if his missing right arm would grow back. It worked, but it also turned him into the Lizard!

The Lizard is very powerful and wants to turn everyone in the world into scaly green creatures like him. He hates Spider-Man for trying to foil his plans, and has often tried to destroy him. Spider-Man has helped turn the Lizard back into Doctor Connors, but the monster is never gone for long.

Sometimes, Connors' mind can control the Lizard's body, but sometimes it is the other way around. Each one tries to overpower the other, and both are always in there somewhere!

While Doctor Connors has long been a friend of Spider-Man, Professor Miles Warren missed his chance to become a good friend of Peter Parker. Instead, the man who seemed to be just another of Peter's professors grew to hate both Peter and Spider-Man. He renamed himself the Jackal, and dedicated himself to destroying the wall-crawler—unusually, by making more of him!

The Jackal blamed Spider-Man for his own unhappiness and tricked other villains into fighting him. When he found out that Peter was Spider-Man, he used Peter's DNA to make a clone—an exact copy of Spidey—to face the real one in battle.

The pair did battle, and afterward it seemed as if the clone and the Jackal had been destroyed in an explosion. Yet both of them had survived, and when the Jackal returned, he was able

to convince Peter that the clone was the real Spider-Man, and that Peter himself was the copy!

The Jackal made lots more clones of Peter, and came up with a plan to give everyone Spider-Man's powers. He even tried to create a scary new species of human-spider hybrids. He has cloned himself many times, so it is impossible to know if he is ever really destroyed.

Lots of Spider-Man's enemies are strange, but at least Sandman, Green Goblin, Doc Ock, and the others are all still human—even the Lizard is sometimes! Venom, in its natural form, is a shapeless blob that looks more like a liquid than a living being. Only when Venom joins together with a person does it become a vicious Super Villain.

When Peter first encountered Venom, he thought it was just a new material he could use to make a strong Spider-Man costume.

Peter wore the outfit, but realized it was alive and trying to control him. He managed to break away from the alien, but now it knew all of Spider-Man's secrets, and was very angry!

The alien joined with a man named Eddie Brock, who also hated Spider-Man, and the new being called itself Venom. This creature believed it was a hero—and that Spider-Man had to be destroyed.

Venom and Spidey have fought many times, but just when the web-slinger thought he knew how to handle his alien foe, it became more dangerous than ever. No longer linked to Brock's body, it was free to join with other human hosts.

If Venom is the strangest of Spider-Man's foes, then Morlun is the most mysterious. An energy vampire that has lived for hundreds of years, Morlun survives by draining the life-force from people with super powers. For him, Spider-Man is the perfect meal!

Morlun is far stronger than he looks and never shows any sign of tiring. The first time they fought, Spider-Man realized that Morlun would be impossible to defeat with strength alone. He decided that the only thing to do was to give the vampire what he wanted. So he let Morlun feed on him—but only after flooding his own body with a huge dose of radiation.

Spider-Man's powers meant that he was not harmed, but Morlun could not handle so much radioactivity, and he was defeated.

For a time, Spider-Man believed that Morlun had been destroyed once and for all. In fact, Morlun was revived in secret, and continued to hunt for beings with super powers—along with the rest of his mysterious vampire family, the Inheritors.

Now that Morlun has touched Spider-Man in battle, he can find him wherever he goes. Sooner or later, he is sure to return.

Amazing Allies

Peter can always rely on his friends in times of need—whether they know him as a Super Hero, a scientist, or the closest thing they will ever have to a son.

It is Aunt May, of course, who worries about Peter as if he were her own child—even though she doesn't know that he is Spider-Man! In fact, only a handful of people do know Peter's secret.

Mary Jane "MJ" Watson has been Peter's friend for many years and figured out for herself that he was Spider-Man. She will always keep his secret and has stood by him during tough times. It's hard work sharing Peter's double life, though, and MJ eventually chose to end their friendship so that she could get on with her own life.

Clever scientist Anna Maria Marconi also uncovered Peter's secret. She worked with Peter and the two of them became good friends. After Anna Maria saw a picture of Spider-Man with marks on his body that matched Peter's, she realized the truth. Now the pair run Parker Industries together.

Peter's Super Hero friendships can be even more complicated than those he shares with his loved ones! Consider the example of cat burglar Felicia Hardy, also known as the Black Cat. She started out as Spider-Man's criminal enemy, then turned her back on burglary to become his girlfriend, but is now his sworn enemy again!

Felicia's father had been a famous cat burglar before her, and she had lived an unhappy life ever since he was caught and sent to prison when she was still a child.

She met Spider-Man on the night that she tried to break her father out of jail. Felicia saw that Spider-Man was not so very different from her—except that he wore a

disguise and worked alone in order to fight crime, not to commit it.

Peter saw that there was a good person behind the Black Cat mask, and tried to help her change her ways. They began to battle bad guys together, and became boyfriend and girlfriend—although Felicia was always more interested in Spider-Man than she was in Peter!

The relationship didn't last, and Felicia has since returned to a life of crime. Though she still has some feelings for Spider-Man, she is now out to destroy him.

Home | **Business** | **Science** | **Heroes**

SPIDER-MAN FOILS
PRISON BREAK

PUBLISHED 8 MINUTES AGO   17 COMMENTS   SHARE

Spider-Man clashed with the Super Villain known as the Black Cat last night, during an attempted breakout at Ryker's Island maximum security prison.

The notorious cat burglar appears to be the mastermind behind the attempt, judging by security camera footage seen by the *Daily Bugle*.

In the recording, Spider-Man can be seen fighting with the Black Cat before trying to reason with her. He then allows her to flee the scene before special weapons police officers arrive to restore order.

A member of staff at the prison who did not want to be named said, "If Spider-Man hadn't arrived when he did, the breakout would definitely have been a success. We owe him our thanks, but I don't know why he let the Black Cat go."

Spider-Man was unavailable for comment at time of publication.

OSCORP

ADVANCEMENT IN SCIENCE

We research because we care. Click here to learn more.

Above: CCTV footage shows Spider-Man under attack from the Black Cat.

Related stories:

Green is the new black: get the Goblin look

10 things you never knew about Captain America

Why the Black Cat is still at large—inside scoop!

This weird tip will stop you Hulking out

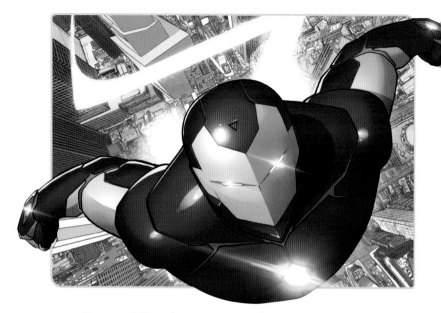

One of Spider-Man's closest Super Hero friends has been billionaire businessman Tony Stark, who doesn't make any secret of his other identity as Iron Man. Just like the web-slinger himself, Tony is an incredibly gifted scientist, and Peter had always looked up to him as an inspiration.

Tony knows that Peter is Spider-Man, and after their paths crossed several times, he knew he could rely on the younger hero. He invited Peter to live in Stark Tower, and offered him a job as his personal assistant.

Tony became Peter's mentor, offering him his take on being a Super Hero. He also made him a suit of armor that looked a lot like Iron Man's! When war broke out between two groups of Super Heroes, Spider-Man had to choose a side. At first, he stood alongside Iron Man, but ended up fighting him instead.

When the war was over, Super Heroes on both sides felt bad about the harm their fighting had caused. They tried to forget their differences and work together again. Peter still sees Iron Man as an important ally, but will not easily call Tony his friend again.

Iron Man is also a vital member of the greatest Super Hero team ever assembled: the Avengers. Spider-Man has fought alongside the Avengers many times, joining forces with Captain America, Thor, Black Widow, Hawkeye, and the Hulk to battle forces that no one hero could beat alone.

Despite their adventures together, the Avengers have not always called Spider-Man a full member of their team. Spidey often prefers to fight alone, and the Avengers do not always agree with how he does things. But when he is really needed, Peter is proud to call himself an Avenger—and they are always happy to help him, too.

When Peter has to rebuild his life after Doc Ock tries to replace him, the Avengers stand by their friend. Captain America and Peter agree that, no matter what, he will always be an Avenger.

AVENGERS CHARTER

We, the Avengers, have banded together to protect the planet Earth, its inhabitants, and its resources from any and all threats that might prove to be beyond the power of conventional forces.

As an Avenger, I will dedicate myself to the establishment, growth, and preservation of:

* Peace
* Liberty
* Equality
* Justice

This is my solemn oath.

Recent global threat: Ultron

Signed:

Peter Parker
....

Witnessed by:

Tony Stark   Steve Rogers
....

CONFIDENTIAL

TEAM MEMBERS

As an Avenger, you will make new enemies, but you will also make new friends. Memorize the following names and details before destroying this document.

Steve Rogers

Natalia Romanova

Me!

CAPTAIN AMERICA is a fearless leader. Exposure to Super-Soldier serum has given him enhanced strength, speed, and healing powers.

IRON MAN is the genius inventor Tony Stark in a high-tech suit of armor. The suit enables him to fly and use many built-in weapons.

BLACK WIDOW is an expert martial artist and a former spy. A version of the Super-Soldier serum keeps her in peak physical condition.

HAWKEYE is an expert archer whose arrows never miss. He doesn't have any super powers, but is skilled in many martial arts.

THOR is an immortal warrior from the realm of Asgard. His indestructible hammer allows him to fly and travel between dimensions.

THE HULK was created in a nuclear accident. He is incredibly strong and fast, can leap huge distances, and is very, very angry.

Call him "Keith"...

Clint Barton

Bruce Banner

Peter, I've written everyone's real names on here, too! - Tony

Spider-Man is also a member of the New Avengers. This team formed to fill the gap that was left behind when the Avengers chose to go their separate ways. But when Captain America brought the Avengers back together, he asked Luke Cage to keep the New Avengers going as an independent team of Super Heroes.

Luke, a very powerful Super Hero with almost unbreakable skin, saw Spider-Man as an obvious choice for his lineup—not least because Spidey had been a part of the team from the beginning. It was not long before Luke and Peter were calling on Ms. Marvel, Mockingbird, and Iron Fist to be part of their crimefighting collective.

When Luke left the New Avengers, he stayed good friends with Peter. When they worked together again, it was as part of a new team—the Mighty Avengers!

Great Responsibilities

Life as Spider-Man is never dull, but some days are much more challenging than others. Spidey's greatest adventures have seen him tested to the limit—fighting against old friends, and struggling to survive against seemingly unstoppable foes.

One of the biggest events to shake Spidey's world was the Superhuman Civil War. The war turned friends into enemies, divided the Avengers team, and saw Spider-Man's identity revealed to the world. It began with a new law that meant all Super Heroes had to tell the United States government who they really were.

Tony Stark made no secret of the fact that he was Iron Man, and he thought the Superhuman Registration Act was a good idea. Tony had helped Peter through some hard times and built him a high-tech new spider suit, so Spider-Man stood alongside Iron Man to support the new law. He even took his mask off in front of a huge crowd to show the whole world who he was.

However, not every Super Hero thought the new law was a good idea. Captain America spoke out against it—and was immediately declared to be an outlaw.

Captain America believed that the Superhuman Registration Act put Super Heroes and their families in unnecessary danger. Some Super Heroes agreed and joined with him to fight against the new law. Soon, other heroes sided with Iron Man and started to hunt down the so-called outlaws.

As the two sides began to fight, Peter saw that he had been wrong to reveal his true identity. If every Super Villain knew that Spider-Man was really Peter Parker, then all the people he loved were now in terrible danger!

Peter turned his back on Iron Man and joined Captain America. It seemed like the fighting would never end, but then Captain America made the most heroic decision of the entire war—he gave up the fight so that no one else would get hurt. Iron Man had won the war, but lost many of his friends.

After the Civil War, Tony Stark learned the dangers of sharing Super Heroes' secrets with the world, and the law was overturned. The magical Doctor Strange made the world forget that Peter was Spider-Man, so his secret identity was safe once more.

THE DIVIDE

When battle lines were drawn between top Avengers, other Super Heroes had to pick a side. Would they support the rule of law with Iron Man, or fight for the freedom to choose alongside Captain America?

CAPTAIN AMERICA

Cap's real name is Steve Rogers, but he believes it is his right to keep that information private if he wants to!

LUKE CAGE

Super-strong Luke goes by his real name, but he believes in the right for everyone to make that choice for themselves.

WICCAN

Billy Kaplan and the other Young Avengers stood with Cap, but they were arrested by Iron Man's forces.

INVISIBLE WOMAN

Sue Richards joined Cap after Iron Man and her husband, Mr. Fantastic, made a dangerous clone of Thor to fight for them.

IRON MAN
The world knows that Tony Stark is Iron Man. He thinks people would be safer if Super Heroes didn't keep secrets.

MS. MARVEL
Before donning her new costume and becoming Captain Marvel, loyal U.S. Air Force officer Carol Danvers backed her government in support of registration.

SHE-HULK
Jennifer Walters is a brilliant lawyer as well as a Super Hero. She believes that all laws should be obeyed.

MR. FANTASTIC
Genius inventor Reed Richards built a Super Hero prison during the Civil War, as well as a violent clone of Thor.

After the Civil War ended, the Avengers reunited to fight Doc Ock and his Super Villain gang, the Sinister Six. Doc Ock convinced the world that he had found a way to stop global warming using special missiles. In reality, he wanted to destroy the planet, leaving just a few survivors to rule over.

When the Avengers tried to stop Ock's plan, he used robots called Octobots to take over their bodies. Only Black Widow and Spider-Man were able to escape. A furious Doc Ock told the world's armies that they would have to destroy Spider-Man to stop global warming.

With the whole world turned against Spider-Man, Peter had to call on allies from the ends of the Earth. He enlisted enough Super Hero friends to launch attacks on all of Doc Ock's missile factories, but the main Avengers were still controlled by Octobots.

Spidey convinced Mysterio to betray the rest of the Sinister Six and help him to save the world. The Super Villain freed the Avengers—allowing them to help Spider-Man destroy the missiles and defeat the Sinister Six.

After his failure to destroy the world, Doctor Octopus did succeed in destroying Peter Parker, seemingly forever. Using an Octobot to replace Peter's mind with his own, Doc Ock began a new life inside Spidey's body. He called himself the Superior Spider-Man, because he thought he could use Peter's powers better than Peter could!

As Spider-Man, Doc Ock tried to continue his criminal ways—even forming a new Sinister Six team. However, he was surprised to find himself doing heroic things, too. This was because Peter's mind still existed deep inside him. Ock even fell in love with Anna Maria Marconi. When she ended up in danger, he realized that Peter was the only one who could save her. He gave up his control of Spidey, and admitted that Peter really was the best Spider-Man.

World of Spiders

Spider-Man has inspired his fair share of imitators over the years. Some are out to do good, but others use their spider skills for evil.

When the Jackal made a perfect copy of Spider-Man, the real Spidey fought him (see p.50). Everyone thought the clone was destroyed, but when Aunt May was unwell, two Peter Parkers turned up to visit her!

The clone had come back because he had all the same memories as the real Peter. He wanted to do good and called himself Ben Reilly—or the Scarlet Spider when he was in his very own spider suit.

Peter began to think of Ben as a brother. The Green Goblin even convinced Peter that Ben was the real Spidey and Peter was the clone. Ben fought the Goblin, but was turned to dust—which proved to Peter that Ben had been the clone all along.

After Ben, another clone of Peter named Kaine became the Scarlet Spider. He struggled to live a good life as a clone, but eventually became a hero.

Thirteen years after he became Spider-Man, Peter met someone who was bitten by the same spider as he was. Cindy Moon has similar powers to Peter, but can also shoot webs straight from her fingertips. She hid herself away for years to avoid Morlun (see p.54), but Spider-Man rescued her when he thought Morlun was dead. Cindy took the Super Hero name Silk and has since helped Spidey battle villains such as Electro—and the very much alive Morlun!

While Cindy Moon spent years waiting to become Silk, Jessica Drew was destined to be Spider-Woman since before she was born. Her parents were both scientists working with spiders and radiation, and their lab tests affected their unborn child.

Jessica grew up to have super strength and speed, and was tricked into joining the criminal gang Hydra. Yet Spider-Woman rejected life as a Super Villain to become a private detective.

She went on to join the Avengers, and fought alongside Spider-Man in the battle against Morlun.

Not every spider-like being is as friendly as Spider-Man. The creature known as Carnage is an alien version of Peter, formed when a drop of  ooze from Venom touched a man named Cletus Kasady. Cletus was a violent criminal even before he was transformed, but with a dose of the Venom alien inside him, he gained its hatred of Spidey, too.

Since Venom used to be linked with Spider-Man, Carnage looks like a twisted take on the Super Hero and can create his own weird webs. Spider-Man has clashed with Carnage many times, and even joined forces with Venom to defeat him. No matter how often Carnage is overcome, he always comes back to cause more chaos.

The villain known as Spider-Slayer did not share any of Spidey's powers but spent his life trying to beat him. The son of a scientist who built "spider slaying" machines, Alastair Smythe wore a robotic suit so that he could become the Ultimate Spider-Slayer.

His fight against Spidey ended when he made the mistake of attacking the Superior Spider-Man, also known as Doctor Octopus.

Doc Ock did not have Spidey's mercy, and so the Spider-Slayer was destroyed.

SPIDER-VERSE HEROES

The Multiverse is home to many versions of planet Earth. Some are very similar to our own, and some are very different, but almost every one has its own version of Spider-Man.

SPIDER-UK
Name: Billy Braddock
Home world: Earth-833
Every version of Earth has a hero to guard the Multiverse. In Peter's world, it is Captain Britain. On Earth-833, it was Spider-UK.

ULTIMATE SPIDER-MAN
Name: Miles Morales
Home world: Earth-1610
A spider that had been injected with a compound containing Peter Parker's blood bit Miles, giving him superhuman powers.

SPIDER-MAN INDIA
Name: Pavitr Prabhakar
Home world: Earth-50101
Pavitr protects the Indian city of Mumbai using spider powers given to him by a mysterious old man.

SPIDER-GWEN
Name: Gwen-Stacey
Home world: Earth-65
In Peter's world, Gwen Stacey was once his girlfriend, but on Earth-65, she is the one who has spider powers!

SP//DR
Name: Peni Parker
Home world: Unknown
Peni allowed herself to be bitten by a radioactive spider so that she could control a special suit of spider armor.

COSMIC SPIDER-MAN
Name: Peter Parker
Home world: Earth-13
This version of Peter Parker gained extra powers from a mysterious outer-space entity called the Enigma Force.

SPIDER-MAN 2099
Name: Miguel O'Hara
Home world: Earth-928
Miguel is a scientist from the year 2099. His world is a future version of Peter Parker's own Earth.

When Spidey learned that Morlun was
still alive, he joined forces with spider Super
Heroes from other realities. Morlun and the
Inheritors could cross the barriers between
universes, so the only way to fight them was
for Spidey to do the same. He visited other
versions of Earth and found that each one
had its own version of Spider-Man—some
of which were very different from him.
The other Spideys wanted Peter to become
their leader, because he was the only one of
them who had ever defeated an Inheritor.

Spider-Man, Silk, Spider-Woman, and
the assembled heroes of the "Spider-verse"
did battle with the Inheritors across many
different worlds. In their final showdown,
Morlun was defeated when Spidey sent him
to a world where the radiation was strong
enough to sap his powers.

Soon, all the Inheritors were banished
to this radioactive prison. The brave spider
heroes all went back to their own realities,
leaving Earth once more in the care of its
friendly neighborhood Spider-Man.

Quiz

1. What is the first name of Peter Parker's aunt?

2. What power lets Peter know when danger is near?

3. How much weight can Spider-Man lift?

4. John Jonah Jameson hired Peter as a photographer for which newspaper?

5. What is the name of the company where Peter is the boss?

6. What is the Green Goblin's real name?

7. What is the name of Doc Ock's gang?

8. What is the full name of Peter's friend MJ?

9. Who made Peter a suit of armor similar to Iron Man's?

10. What gives Captain America his powers?

11. Which Super Villain told the world he could stop global warming?

12. What is Jennifer Walters' Super Hero name?

13. True or false: Silk uses web shooters like Spider-Man's.

14. Who was the Spider-Slayer?

15. What name is Miguel O'Hara also known by?

See page 95 for answers.

Glossary

Absorb
Soak up one thing inside another, like water in a sponge.

Ally or Allies
Friend or friends.

Billionaire
Someone with more than one billion dollars.

Cat burglar
A thief that moves as carefully and as quietly as a cat.

Clone
An exact copy of a person or thing.

Concentration
Thinking about just one thing.

Encouraged
Gave help and support.

Ferocious
Wild and strong.

Foe
An enemy.

Glimpse
A quick look.

Government
A group of people allowed to make laws and rules.

Havoc
Destruction and disorder.

Hijack
To take control of something without permission.

Hybrid
A mix of two different things.

Indestructible
Something that can't be destroyed.

Inspiration
A thing or person that influences you or sparks ideas for you.

Laboratory
A place where scientists work, also called a lab.

Mentor
Someone who gives training and advice.

Outlaw
Someone living in a way that goes against the rules.

Puny
Small and weak.

Radioactivity
A kind of energy that can be very dangerous in large amounts.

Reflexes
Actions your body make without thinking.

Reptiles
Animals with cold blood and scaly skin, such as snakes.

Responsibility
A job that you have to do.

Sinister
Creepy and evil.

Vibration
Very fast shaking movements.

Index

Alastair Smythe 85
Aleksei Sytsevich 45
Anna Maria Marconi 57, 78
Aunt May 6, 7, 16, 19, 21, 43, 56, 80
Avengers 64–67, 69, 70, 76, 77, 83
Avengers Academy 33
Ben Reilly 81
Billy Braddock 86
Billy Kaplan 74
Black Cat 58–59, 60, 61
Black Widow 64, 67, 76
Bruce Banner 67 see also Hulk
Captain America 61, 64, 67, 69, 71, 72, 73, 74
Captain Britain 86
Carnage 84
Carol Danvers see also Ms. Marvel 75
Chameleon 45
Cindy Moon 82, 83
Cletus Cassidy 84
Clint Barton 67 see also Hawkeye
Cosmic Spider-Man 87
Daily Bugle 20–21, 29, 30–31, 60–61
Dmitri Smerdyakov 45
Doctor Curt Connors 48–49, 50 see also Lizard
Doctor Octopus 19, 33, 42–43, 44, 46, 52, 57, 64, 76, 77, 78, 85
Doctor Strange 73
Earth-13 87
Earth-65 87
Earth-833 86
Earth-928 87
Earth-1610 86
Earth-50101 86
Eddie Brock 53
Electro 20, 41, 42, 45, 82
Empire State University 32
Enigma Force 87

Felicia Hardy 58, 59 see also Black Cat
Flash 21
Green Goblin 36–37, 38, 41, 52, 61, 81
Gwen Stacey 87
Harry Osborn 38, 39
Hawkeye 64, 67
Horizon Labs 32, 33
Hulk 64, 67
Hydra 83
Inheritors 55, 88, 89
Invisible Woman 74
Iron Fist 69
Iron Man 62–63, 64, 67, 71, 72, 73, 74, 75
Jackal 50–51, 80
Jennifer Walters 75
Jessica Drew 83 see also Spider-Woman
John Jonah Jameson 21, 28, 29, 30
Kaine 81
Lizard 27, 48–49, 52
Luke Cage 69, 74
Mary Jane "MJ" Watson 57
Maxwell Dillon 41, 42, 45 see also Electro
Midtown High School 6, 8
Mighty Avengers 69
Miguel O'Hara 87
Miles Morales 86
Mockingbird 69
Morlun 54–55, 82, 83, 88, 89
Mr. Fantastic 74, 75
Ms. Marvel 69, 75
Multiverse 86–87
Mysterio 44, 77
Natalia Romanova 67 see also Black Widow
New Avengers 69
Norman Osborn 36–37, 38, 39, 41 see also Green Goblin

Octobots 76, 77, 78
Oscorp 38–39, 61
Otto Octavius 42, 44 *see also*
    Doctor Octopus
Peni Parker 87
Parker Industries 33, 57
Pravitr Prabhakar 86
Professor Miles Warren 50
Quentin Beck 44
Raymond Warren 8
Reed Richards 75
Rhino 45
Ryker's Island Prison 60
Sandman 19, 45, 46–47, 48, 52
Scarlet Spider 81
She-Hulk 75
Silk 82, 83, 89
Sinister Six 43, 44–45, 46, 76,
    77, 78
SP/DR 87
Spider-Gwen 87
Spider-Man 2099 87
Spider-Man India 86
spider-sense 22, 23
Spider-Slayer 85
spider suit 13, 14, 15, 19, 23, 24–25,
    34–35
Spider-UK 86
Spider-Woman 83, 89
Stark Tower 62
Steve Rogers 66, 67, 74 *see also*
    Captain America

Sue Richards 74
Superhuman Civil War 63, 70–75,
    76
Superhuman Registration Act
    71, 72
Super-Soldier serum 67, 86
Superior Spider-Man 78, 85
Thor 64, 67, 74, 75
Tony Stark 62, 63, 66, 67, 71, 73, 75
see also Iron Man
Ultimate Spider-Man 86
Ultimate Spider-Slayer 85
Ultron 66
Uncle Ben 6, 7, 16, 19
Venom 52–53, 54, 84
Vulture 19
web shooters 14, 23, 24
Wiccan 74
William Baker 45, 46
    see also Sandman

Quiz answers

1. May 2. Spider-sense
3. Almost 10 tons 4. Daily
Bugle 5. Parker Industries
6. Norman Osborn 7. The
Sinister Six 8. Mary Jane Watson
9. Tony Stark 10. Super-Soldier
serum 11. Doc Ock 12. She-Hulk
13. False—she can shoot webs
from her fingertips 14. Alastair
Smythe 15. Spider-Man 2099

Have you read these other great books from DK?

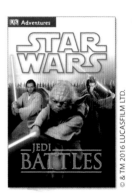

Read all about
the scariest
monsters in the
Star Wars galaxy.

Join the mighty
Avengers as they
battle the power-
mad robot Ultron!

Find out all about
the brave Jedi
Knights and their
epic adventures.

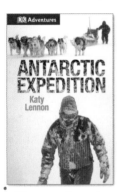

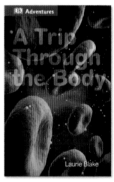

Discover how to
survive in the most
hostile place on
Earth—Antarctica.

Enjoy the myths
and legends from
long ago and
across the world.

Explore the
amazing systems
at work inside the
human body.